Mind The Meteo...

by Alex Woolf
Illustrated by Dan Crisp

Contents

Rocks from Space 2
What Are Meteoroids? 3
What Are Meteors? 4
What Are Meteorites? 8
What Are Asteroids? 10
What Are Comets? 16
Space Rock Summary! 19
Asteroid Craters 20
A Rocky End 22
Hunting for Asteroids 26
How to Stop an Asteroid Hitting Earth 28
Exploring Asteroids 30
Glossary and Index 32

OXFORD
UNIVERSITY PRESS

Rocks from Space

When we look up at the sky, it seems very peaceful. In fact, there are small rocks from outer space falling towards the Earth all the time!

Have you ever seen a shooting star in the sky? These flashes of light are not actually stars – they are space rocks called meteoroids which are falling towards the ground as meteors.

What Are Meteoroids?

Eight planets – including our planet Earth – **orbit** around the Sun. This is our **solar system**.

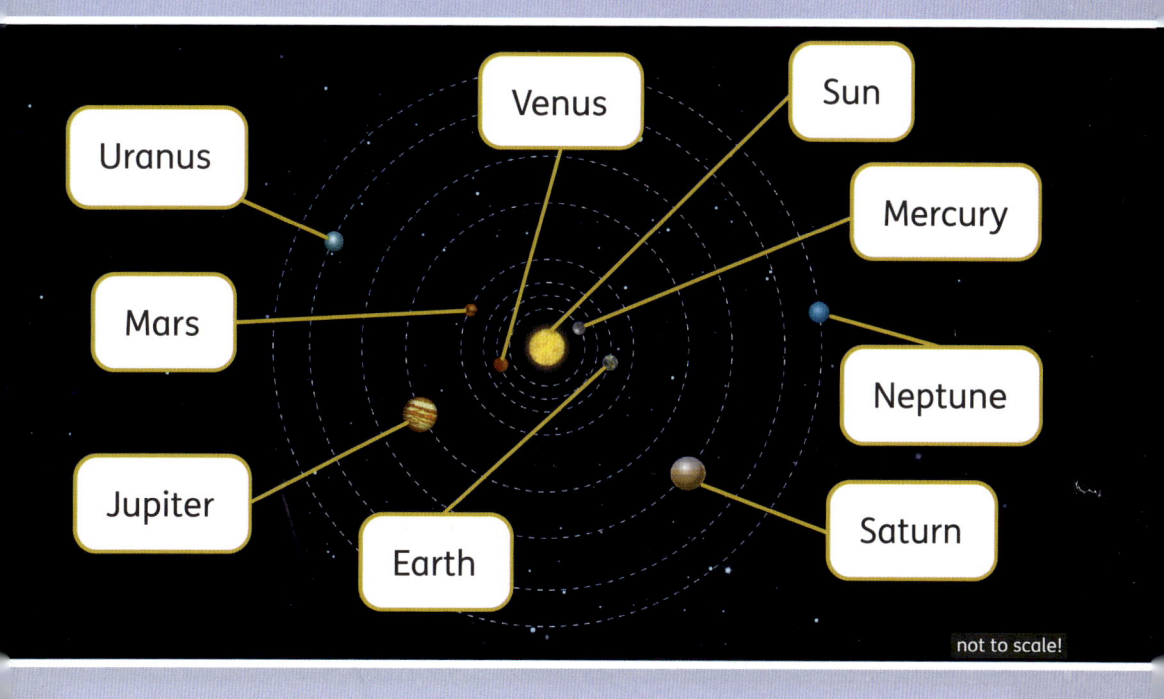

Venus | Sun | Uranus | Mercury | Mars | Neptune | Jupiter | Saturn | Earth

not to scale!

However, there are other, much smaller things in our solar system too. Meteoroids are lumps of rock and metal that also orbit the Sun.

If meteoroids get close enough to a planet, they can stop going around the Sun and begin to fall towards the planet. This is why rocks from space sometimes land on Earth.

What Are Meteors?

When a meteoroid enters Earth's **atmosphere**, it moves so fast that it heats up and starts to glow. Once a meteoroid starts to burn brightly like this, it is called a 'meteor'.

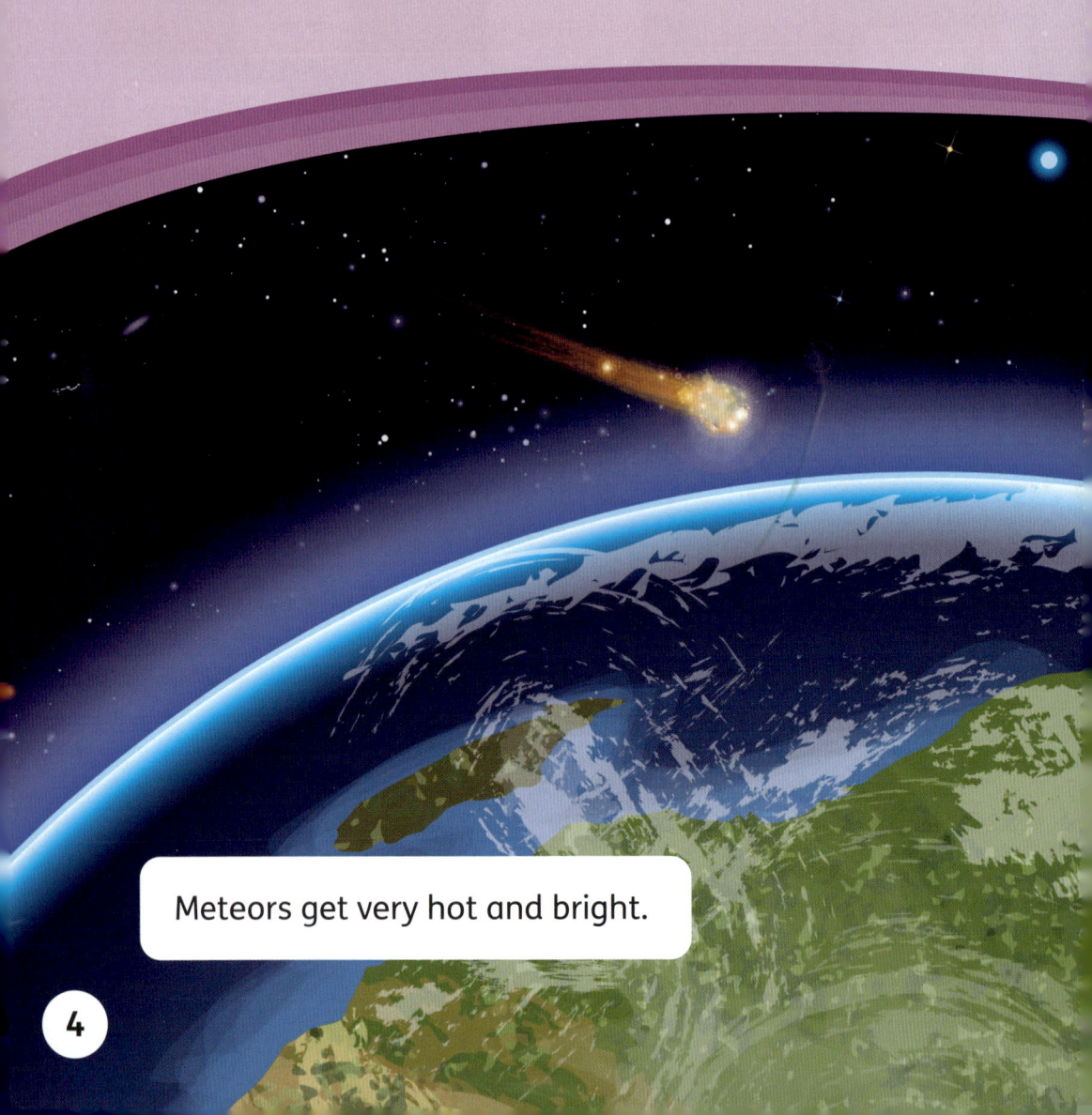

Meteors get very hot and bright.

Every day, millions of meteors fall into Earth's atmosphere. Most of these come from small meteoroids, no bigger than a grain of sand. Meteors are falling all the time but usually they can only be seen at night.

Meteor showers

Sometimes Earth can pass through a big group of meteoroids, causing a meteor 'shower'. The meteors look like hundreds of streaks of light in the night sky.

How can I see meteors?

If you watch the sky at night, you might be lucky and see a meteor!

- Ask an adult to help you find out when a meteor shower will be visible near your home.
- Choose a clear night with no clouds.
- Go with an adult to a safe place without too much light. Street lights make it harder to see the night sky.
- Give your eyes at least fifteen minutes to adjust to seeing in the dark.
- Be patient and watch carefully – meteors can appear anywhere in the sky!

On 10th August 1972, there was a meteor that was bright enough to be seen during the daytime. It appeared above parts of the USA and Canada, and could be seen streaking across the blue sky for 100 seconds.

The Fireball

The meteor was called the Great Daylight Fireball. It didn't fall to the ground but just passed through Earth's atmosphere for a <u>brief</u> time. The closest it came to Earth was 57 kilometres as it passed over Montana, USA.

Fireball

The Fireball passed through Earth's atmosphere for a <u>brief</u> time. Does that mean it was in Earth's atmosphere for a short while or a long while?

What Are Meteorites?

As meteors fall through the Earth's atmosphere, they usually burn up and are destroyed. If any pieces of rock survive and land on Earth, they are known as 'meteorites'. The bigger ones make **craters** where they land.

Many thousands of meteorites have been found over the centuries. The largest meteorite ever found was the Hoba meteorite. It fell to Earth in Namibia and has never been moved, because it weighs 60 tons – that's more than eight elephants!

the Hoba meteorite

Hit by a meteorite!

In the USA in 1954, a woman was sleeping on her sofa when a meteorite crashed through the roof and hit her. It left a nasty bruise on her side but she was otherwise unharmed. Don't worry! This doesn't happen often. In fact it is very <u>rare</u>.

If something is <u>rare</u>, is it very uncommon or does it happen a lot?

What Are Asteroids?

Asteroids are like meteoroids, but much larger. They also orbit the Sun. They can range in size from 1 metre wide to almost the size of a small planet. Unlike round planets, they have an uneven shape. They are made of rocky **minerals** and metals.

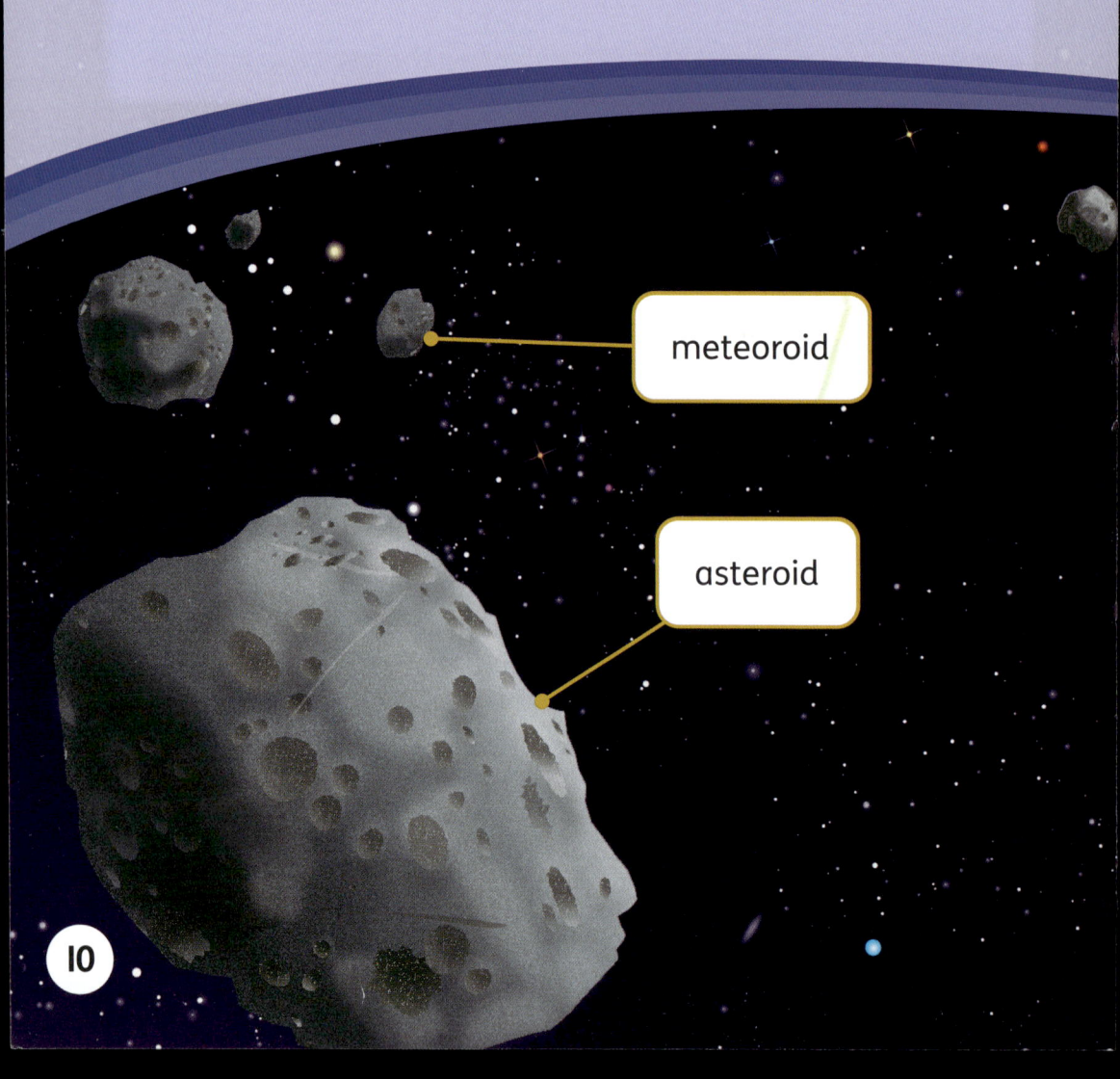

meteoroid

asteroid

How were asteroids formed?

Long ago in our solar system, the Sun was surrounded by gas and dust. Most of this gas and dust stuck together and formed the enormous planets of our solar system. This process took many millions of years. However, some of the gas and dust never became part of a planet. This leftover material stuck together and formed rocky asteroids.

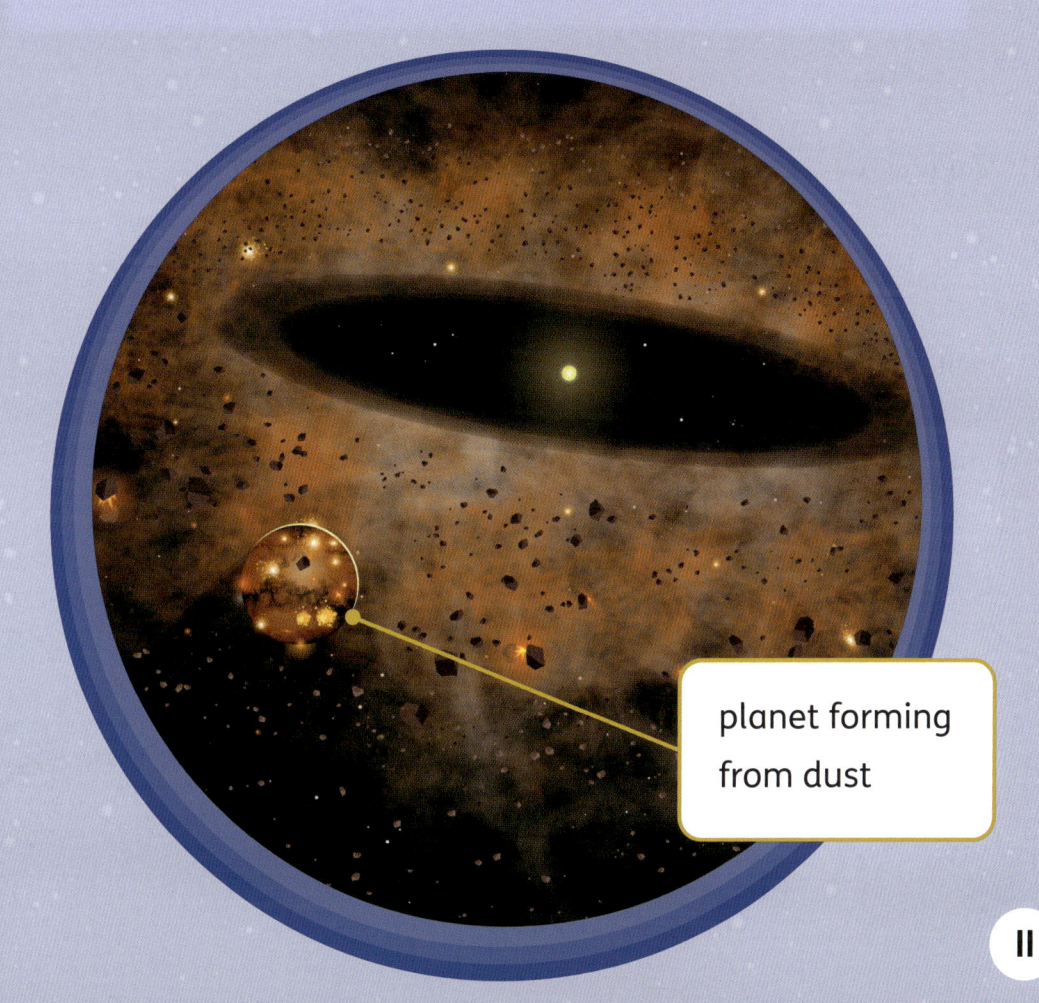

planet forming from dust

The three biggest asteroids are Vesta, Pallas and Hygiea (*say* hi-jee-uh). The biggest asteroids were also the first to be discovered. This is because they were easier to see with early telescopes than smaller asteroids.

Vesta, the largest asteroid, was discovered in 1807 and is 530 kilometres wide. It takes over three and a half Earth-years for Vesta to orbit the Sun. It is also the brightest asteroid and can sometimes be seen from Earth without a telescope!

Vesta

The asteroid belt

Most asteroids, including Vesta, Pallas and Hygiea, lie within the asteroid belt. The asteroid belt is between the orbits of Mars and Jupiter. It contains millions of asteroids.

asteroid belt

Many are very large, but the space they travel through is enormous, and they rarely hit each other. When they do, they break up – creating more asteroids and meteroids.

Near-Earth asteroids

Not all asteroids are in the asteroid belt. Some have orbits that bring them close to Earth. These are called near-Earth asteroids (NEAs). Scientists estimate there are around 20 000 NEAs.

Sometimes these NEAs get so close to the Earth that they begin to fall towards it. Just like meteoroids, when an asteroid enters Earth's atmosphere and begins to burn brightly it is called a 'meteor'.

Asteroid collisions

- Asteroids of 4 metres wide strike us about once a year.
- Asteroids of 20 metres wide hit Earth about once every 50 years.

Fireball in the sky

An asteroid hit the Earth in February 2013. It appeared in the skies above part of Russia and looked like a fast-moving fireball. Observers were <u>astonished</u> by the sight. The fireball exploded, and the resulting **shock wave** damaged hundreds of buildings and injured over 1600 people.

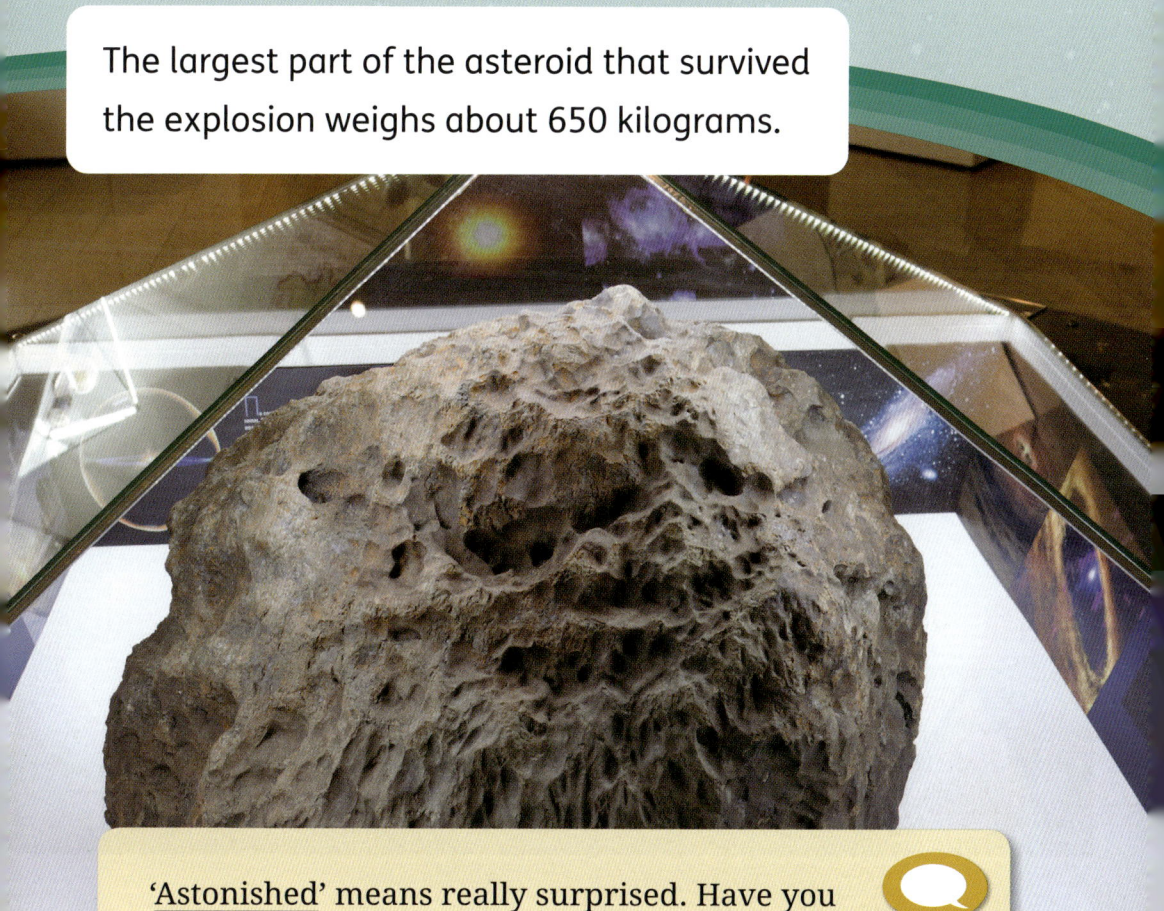

The largest part of the asteroid that survived the explosion weighs about 650 kilograms.

'<u>Astonished</u>' means really surprised. Have you ever been <u>astonished</u> by something you've seen?

What Are Comets?

Asteroids and meteoroids are not the only space objects that can come close to Earth.

Comets are balls of ice, dust and gas that also orbit the Sun. They sometimes have a 'tail' made of dust and gas that can be millions of kilometres long. These tails can often be seen from Earth.

a comet

The mysterious flattened forest

On the morning of 30th June 1908, there was a huge explosion in Siberia, Russia. It flattened over 2000 square kilometres of forest, and destroyed around 80 million trees.

For a long time there were not many <u>details</u> about what had happened, but now most experts believe the 'Tunguska event' was caused by a large object from space.

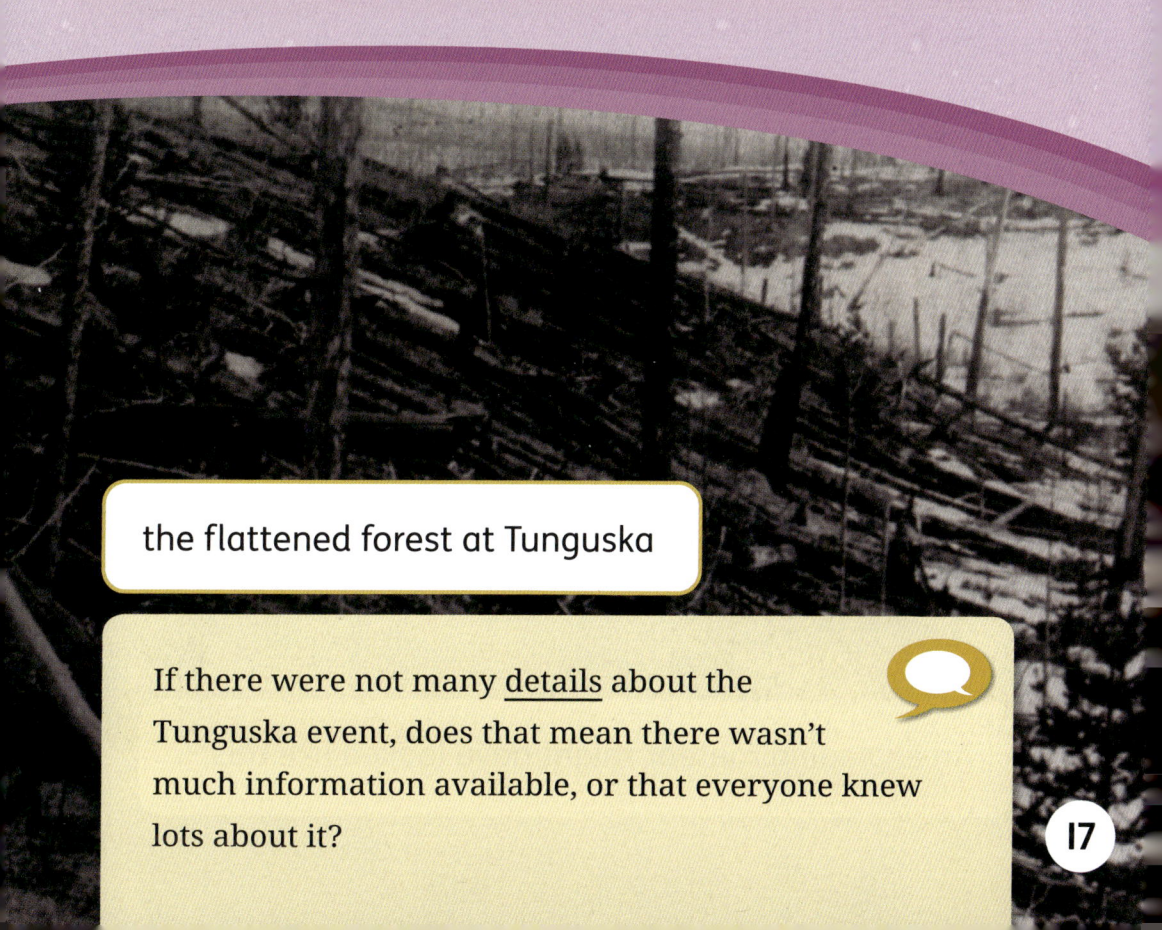

the flattened forest at Tunguska

If there were not many <u>details</u> about the Tunguska event, does that mean there wasn't much information available, or that everyone knew lots about it?

The Tunguska event: asteroid or comet?

Whatever caused the Tunguska event, it didn't leave a crater. There are several theories about what could have flattened the forest but left no other trace.

It could have been a comet: they are made of ice and dust and might not make a crater. It could have been a meteor exploding in the air without hitting the ground. Some scientists think it was an iron asteroid 100 metres wide that grazed Earth's atmosphere without landing.

An exploding meteor might have looked like this.

Space Rock Summary!

There are lots of types of space rocks and it can be difficult to remember them! This table summarizes all the different space rocks that you have read about.

Image	Name	What is it?
	comet	a lump of ice, dust and gas that orbits the Sun
	asteroid	a large rocky object, bigger than a meteoroid but smaller than a planet, that orbits the Sun
	meteoroid	a small chunk of rock or metal that orbits the Sun
	meteor	a rock that is falling through the Earth's atmosphere and burning bright and hot – may have been a meteoroid or an asteroid
	meteorite	a rock that survives the journey through the Earth's atmosphere and lands on Earth

Asteroid Craters

Over its long history, Earth has suffered from the **impact** of some big asteroids, which have left craters in its landscape. One of the best examples is the Barringer crater in Arizona, USA.

49 000 years ago, a huge asteroid 30–50 metres wide hit the ground and caused a massive explosion. The crater it made is so deep you could stack 38 double-decker buses inside it!

One of the biggest asteroid craters on Earth is the Chicxulub (*say* chix-u-loob) crater in Mexico. It is 180 kilometres wide.

It was formed by a giant asteroid that struck the Earth around 66 million years ago. The asteroid was at least 11 kilometres wide.

You cannot see the crater, but scientists can detect it and make pictures like this to show its size.

A rocky end?

Some scientists believe it was the Chicxulub asteroid impact that caused the extinction of the dinosaurs, as this also happened about 66 million years ago. The impact of the Chicxulub asteroid would have set off a chain of disasters: earthquakes, fires and floods.

The atmosphere would have been clogged with millions of tons of dust, blocking out sunlight for many months. During this period, little food would grow, so the dinosaurs may have died of starvation.

Impact winter

Without sunlight, plants die, and so do the animals that feed on the plants. This period is known as an 'impact winter'.

Then the sun gradually reappears and things return to normal.

If the sun gradually appears, does it appear quickly or slowly?

✦ Underwater craters ✦

Large craters have even been found on the floor of the ocean. Scientists think that they were formed when comets or asteroids hit the water and plunged right down to the seabed. There would have been an enormous splash!

Asteroids are much more likely to fall into the ocean than on to land, because 70% of Earth's surface is covered in water.

Growing food without sunlight

If an asteroid did strike, people would find ways to survive. With so little sunlight, it could be difficult to keep a supply of food. People might have to grow plants for food indoors, using special lighting instead of sunlight.

Big asteroid impacts are extremely rare! They happen once every few *million* years, so it's very unlikely you'll experience one in your lifetime.

Other than food, what would you gather a supply of if you knew an asteroid was about to strike next month?

Hunting for Asteroids

The dinosaurs didn't have telescopes! They didn't see their asteroid coming. We will be better prepared. **Astronomers** around the world are constantly watching the skies, searching for NEAs and comets that might pose a problem.

Larger asteroids (over 100 metres) can be seen from a long way off. Astronomers can work out if they are likely to hit Earth.

an asteroid's orbit crossing the Earth's orbit

not to scale!

Smaller asteroids

Asteroids that are smaller than 100 metres are much more common than big ones. They are a bit harder to spot until they are close. Therefore, systems have been set up to keep watch for them.

The ATLAS system

One of these is ATLAS, an asteroid early-warning system in Hawaii, USA. It sends signals to warn scientists about approaching asteroids a few weeks or days before they get near Earth.

ATLAS is based in two **observatories**.

Can you name any other situations where we need to use signals? Think about transport, or communicating with others.

How to Stop an Asteroid Hitting Earth

Suppose we see a big asteroid heading towards Earth. What can we do about it? Experts believe we could prevent it from striking our planet.

One method would be to send a very heavy spacecraft called a 'gravity tractor' to the asteroid. If it got close to the asteroid, it might be able to pull it into a different orbit. However, it could take several years to change the asteroid's orbit.

This is what a gravity tractor might look like.

A quicker solution would be for a heavy spacecraft to ram the asteroid. If it struck the asteroid with enough force, it could push it away from Earth.

A third option would be to set off an explosion near the asteroid, shattering it into pieces.

Exploring Asteroids

Humans haven't just studied asteroids through telescopes. We have also sent spacecraft to visit them.

The first mission was in 1991 when the American spacecraft Galileo (*say* gal-ill-ay-oh) flew past an asteroid called Gaspara. In 2005, the Japanese spacecraft Hayabusa (*say* hi-ah-boo-sa) was the first to land on an asteroid. It touched down on the asteroid Itokawa (*say* ee-toe-kah-wah) and collected a sample of dust.

Hayabusa spacecraft

Asteroids contain many useful metals, including cobalt, iron and nickel. Some scientists believe that in the future we could use asteroids as a source of these metals. A spacecraft might even <u>seize</u> the asteroid and take it to a safe orbit around the Moon or Earth so we can build a mine on it.

At the moment, asteroids are simply interesting objects in the sky. Maybe one day we could make use of them.

Mining asteroids could be the future!

Spacecraft might be able to <u>seize</u> asteroids. Can you think of another word or phrase that could be used instead of '<u>seize</u>'?

Glossary

astronomers: scientists who study the stars, planets and other objects in space
atmosphere: the gases that surround the Earth
craters: holes in the ground made by something falling or exploding
impact: the action of one object crashing into another, or a strong effect on something
minerals: solid substances that form naturally, like salt
observatories: buildings with telescopes for looking into space
orbit: to go around something; the curved path of an object or spacecraft round a star, planet, or moon
shock wave: a sharp change in pressure caused by an explosion or impact

Index

asteroid belt	13
Barringer crater	13
Chicxulub crater	21–22
dinosaurs	22–23
Great Daylight Fireball	7
Hoba meteorite	8
meteor showers	5
solar system	3, 10–11, 13